I0439114

OCS Report
MMS 2009-018

Investigation of Fatal Fall from Rig Pollution Pan
Galveston Area Block 151, Well No. 6
OCS-G 15740
28 January 2008

Gulf of Mexico
Off the Texas Coast

U.S. Department of the Interior
Minerals Management Service
Gulf of Mexico OCS Regional Office

OCS Report
MMS 2009-018

Investigation of Fatal Fall from Rig Pollution Pan
Galveston Area Block 151, Well No. 6
OCS-G 15740
28 January 2008

Gulf of Mexico
Off the Texas Coast

Jack Williams – Chair
Tom Perry
Craig Pohler
Glynn Breaux

U.S. Department of the Interior
Minerals Management Service
Gulf of Mexico OCS Regional Office

New Orleans
March 2009

Contents

Executive Summary

On 28 January 2008, a fatal accident occurred on Hercules Offshore (Hercules) Rig 251, Galveston Area Block 151, Lease OCS-G 15740, in the Gulf of Mexico, offshore Texas.

Hall-Houston, the operator, had contracted Hercules Offshore to conduct well work that included installing a 60-inch over-drive caisson over a well. In the course of that operation, two welders from Frank's Casing Crews (Frank's) began cutting a hole in the pollution pan big enough to allow the passage of the drive pipe caisson.

While cutting the hole, the welders also cut several apparently extraneous 3-inches wide metal straps welded to the floor of the pollution pan and to the sub-structure support beams. When the last of the straps were cut, the pollution pan suddenly dropped away from beneath the welders, landing on the Texas deck 50-feet (ft) below the rig floor. One of the welders was unable get out of the pan when it dropped. He was fatally injured in the resulting fall.

The Panel investigation concluded the pollution pan was only held in place by the metal straps. It was not hard-welded or securely bolted to the sub-structure as is usual on most rigs. Fall protection was not used by the welders because the Frank's supervisor had an erroneous understanding of how the pan was attached. None of the other Frank's personnel knew that cutting the straps would allow the pan to fall. The Hercules personnel who knew how the pan was secured thought they were ones responsible for removal of the pan. However, that responsibility was not made clear to the Frank's personnel.

No mandatory JSA meeting attended by both Hercules and Frank's personnel had been held prior to the start of the job to discuss the removal of the oil pan. The Hercules personnel on the rig floor did not know who the Frank's supervisor was. Communication between the Offshore Installation Manager (OIM), Frank's, and Hercules personnel was confusing, contradictory and incomplete. Even an attempt to invoke a "stop work authority" failed due to confusing and unclear methodology specified in the manual.

It is possible that fatigue played a role in the misunderstandings that led to this accident.

Introduction

Authority

A fatal accident (the Accident) occurred on *28 January 2008* at approximately *0733 hours* (hrs) aboard the jack-up drilling rig Hercules Offshore (Hercules or the Rig Company) Rig 251 (the Rig) contracted to Hall Houston Exploration Company (Operator or H-H) while operations were being conducted for the Operator on Lease OCS-G 15740, Galveston Area Block 151 (GA-151), Well No. 6 (the Well), in the Gulf of Mexico, offshore Texas.

The fatally injured person (Welder #1) was an employee of the contractor specialty casing company, Frank's Casing Crews (Frank's or the Contractor). The Welder #1 was cutting a hole in the oil pollution prevention pan (Oil Pan) beneath the Rig floor as part of preparations to run 60-inch (in) diameter over-drive caisson pipe when the Accident occurred.

Pursuant to 43 U.S.C. 1348(d)(1) and (2) and (f) [Outer Continental Shelf (OCS) Lands Act, as amended] and Department of the Interior regulations 30 CFR 250, the Minerals Management Service (MMS) is required to investigate and prepare a public report of this accident. By memorandum dated February 1, 2008, personnel were named to the investigative panel, with an additional member added on June 9, 2008, to include the following:

> Jack Williams, Chairman – Office of Safety Management, GOM OCS Region;
> Tom Perry – Offshore Regulatory Program, Accident Enforcement Branch, OMM, Herndon;
> Craig Pohler – District Engineer, Lake Jackson District, Field Operations OCS Region.
> Glynn Breaux – Office of Safety Management, GOM OCS Region;

Background

Lease OCS-G 15740 (the Lease) covers approximately 4804 acres (ac), that acreage seaward of the State of Texas-U. S. boundary, and is located in Galveston Area Block 151, Gulf of Mexico, off the Texas Coast (*see figure 1*). The Lease was purchased in Sale 155 by equal interest owners comprised of Mariner Energy Inc., El Paso E&P Company L.P. and Eni Petroleum US LLC. Pisces Energy Co. LLC later acquired El Paso's interest. Mariner currently is operator of record for the lease.

Operator rights designation for the Southwest one-quarter of the Lease (approximately 1, 250-ac), from the surface to 8,910-ft, was assigned to Hall-Houston Exploration II, LP (Operator) – 65%, Peregrine Oil and Gas II, LLC – 33%, and RTR Fund I, LP – 2%. Hall-Houston is the Operator of Record for this area.

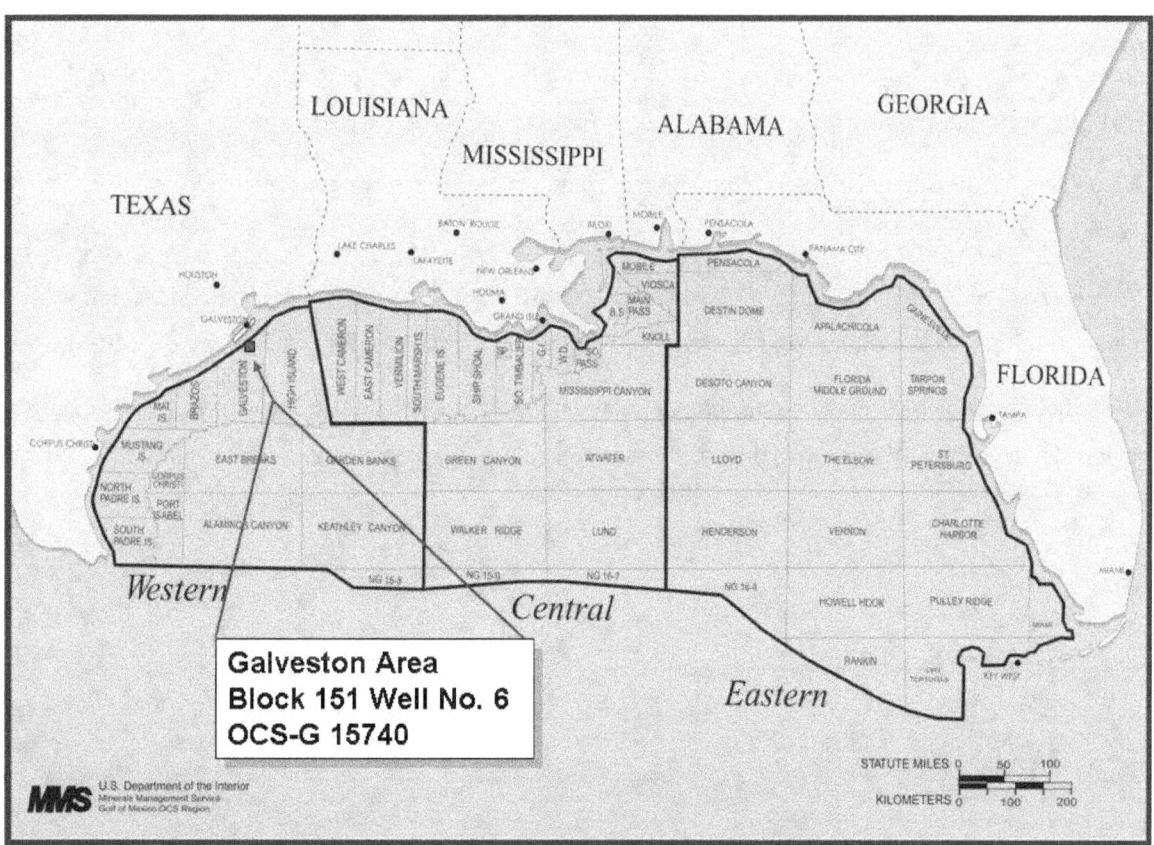

Figure 1 – Location of Lease OCS-G 15740, Galveston Area Block 151, Well No. 6

Procedures

28 January 2008: The Minerals Management Service (MMS) Lake Jackson District office was notified of the accident by Operator;

1 February 2008: A MMS Regional Director letter assigned Panel members to investigate the Accident.

3 March 2008: The initial Panel meeting was conducted to discuss investigation methodology. Relevant information was requested from Operator, Rig Company and Contractor;

9 June 2008: The MMS Panel was revised to include an additional member;

July, 2008: An accident summary was prepared from the initial accident data, and distributed for Panel review and requests for additional data were forwarded to the companies.

July-August, 2008: Requested data was received from Contractor, Operator and Rig Company.

August, 2008: Formal witness interviews were conducted by Panel members with Frank's personnel at the MMS Lafayette District office;

September, 2008: Additional interviews with Rig Company personnel were conducted by Panel members;

November, 2008: Telephone interviews with additional Rig Company personnel were conducted by two members of the Panel. Additional data covering Frank's and Hercules safety policies were received.

The Panel members met several times throughout the investigation to conduct interviews, discuss and review the data and testimony, and draw necessary conclusions to prepare this report.

Findings

Activities – Timeline through the Accident

In *January, 2008*, the Rig was preparing to run 60-inch drive pipe over the Well as part of the construction of a stand-alone caisson to support equipment enabling the Well to begin production.

Hercules contracted Frank's to run the 60-inch drive pipe as that operation involving pipe of that diameter usually requires specialty expertise and equipment. The Contractor, Frank's, sent eight personnel to conduct the operation. These included one supervisor (the Welding Supervisor), one hammer operator (the Hammer Operator) and six welders. The Frank's personnel were organized into two 12 hour shifts and were intending to work around the clock until completion of the job.

The Frank's crew arrived on the Rig at approximately *2300-hrs 27 Jan* after a 10 hour boat trip. Upon arriving on the Rig, the Frank's personnel were briefed on the safety aspects of the Rig and were assigned muster stations in the event emergency evacuation became necessary.

0000-0700 28 Jan: The Hercules Rig crew prepared for the upcoming drive pipe operation by removing V-door posts and handrails, removing the rotary table, and washing out the pollution pan.

0500-hrs, 28 Jan: Removal of the rotary table was completed by the Rig crew. This exposed a 12-ft x 9-ft x 6-ft deep "well" beneath the rotary table (the Rotary Table Well), bottoming on the top of the Oil Pan, (*see figure 2*). The Franks crew then was mobilized to prepare to run the 60-inch drive pipe.

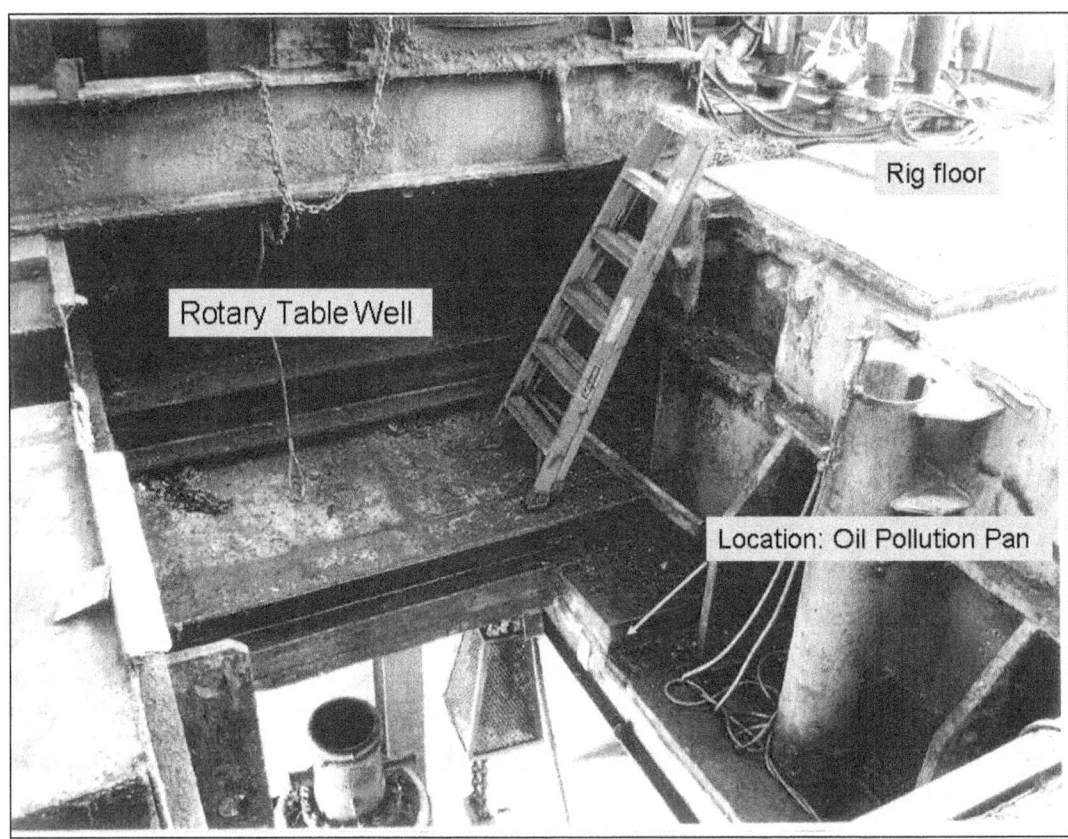

Figure 2 – Rotary table well and location of oil pollution pan

0500-hrs, 28 Jan: The Rig manager on duty (Night Tool Pusher) and the Driller conducted a JSA-think plan-safety meeting for Hercules personnel to discuss the upcoming over-drive operation. None of the Frank's personnel attended the meeting and a signed JSA was not completed indicating the agenda and the attendees. While most of the Rig personnel on-tower attended, some Hercules personnel were not at the meeting as attendance was not mandatory.

A Rig JSA think plan form was generated some period of time after the meeting was held. The Think Plan form was later signed off on by one of the Frank's personnel, the Hammer Operator. The think plan noted "*the installation of the false rotary beams required cutting out the floor plates, installing the cross beams and then... [the] ...'rotary pan is to be cut out and removed.'*" The think plan indicated that the welding equipment, torches, needleguns, hammers, air hoists, etc., had been inspected by the Driller, and that safety belts and fall devices were available and inspected. No details of the method to be used to remove the Oil Pan were included in the Rig think plan.

6

0500-hrs, 28 Jan: A short meeting separate from the Rig JSA was held for the Frank's crew by the Franks Welding Supervisor. The meeting primarily focused on the pipe running operation and the assignments for each of the Frank's crew during that operation were discussed. No detailed discussion was held about preparation of the Rig floor, installation of the beams, etc.   From testimony, no drawings of the rig floor (*see figure 3, p. 8, and figure 4, p. 9*) were available during the discussion, nor was there any discussion about the specifics involving the removal of the Oil Pan.

0600-hrs: The shifts of the Rig managers changed with the OIM taking over from the Night Tool Pusher. Two men from Rig descended to the Texas deck some 50-ft below the Rig floor to check on the status of the well head. Operations continued on the Rig floor.

The OIM walked onto the Rig floor and engaged the Frank's Welding Supervisor in conversation for approximately 10-20 minutes. They discussed the general aspects of the job and requirements to successfully complete the overdrive. Shortly thereafter, the Driller realized that the hot work permit had not been properly signed and he approached the Hammer Operator who signed the form.

0700-hrs: Cutting the Rig floor beams and support collars to allow the installation of the false rotary beams was completed by the Frank's crew. Two welders of Frank's crew, Welder #1 and Welder #2, descended into the bottom of the Rotary Table Well to cut out a portion of the Oil Pan large enough to allow the passage of the 60-inch over-drive pipe.

The 39-inch diameter opening for the rotary in the Oil Pan itself was covered with an unsecured pallet to prevent falls onto the Texas Deck some 50-ft below. Though the Rotary Table Well was 6-ft deep, no fall protection was worn by the two welders, nor any of the other personnel working in the area of the Rotary Table Well.

Seeing the two Frank's personnel beginning to cut the Oil Pan the Driller approached the Frank's Hammer Operator and told him not to cut the Oil Pan until he [the Driller] was ready. He did not give a reason for his instruction at that time.

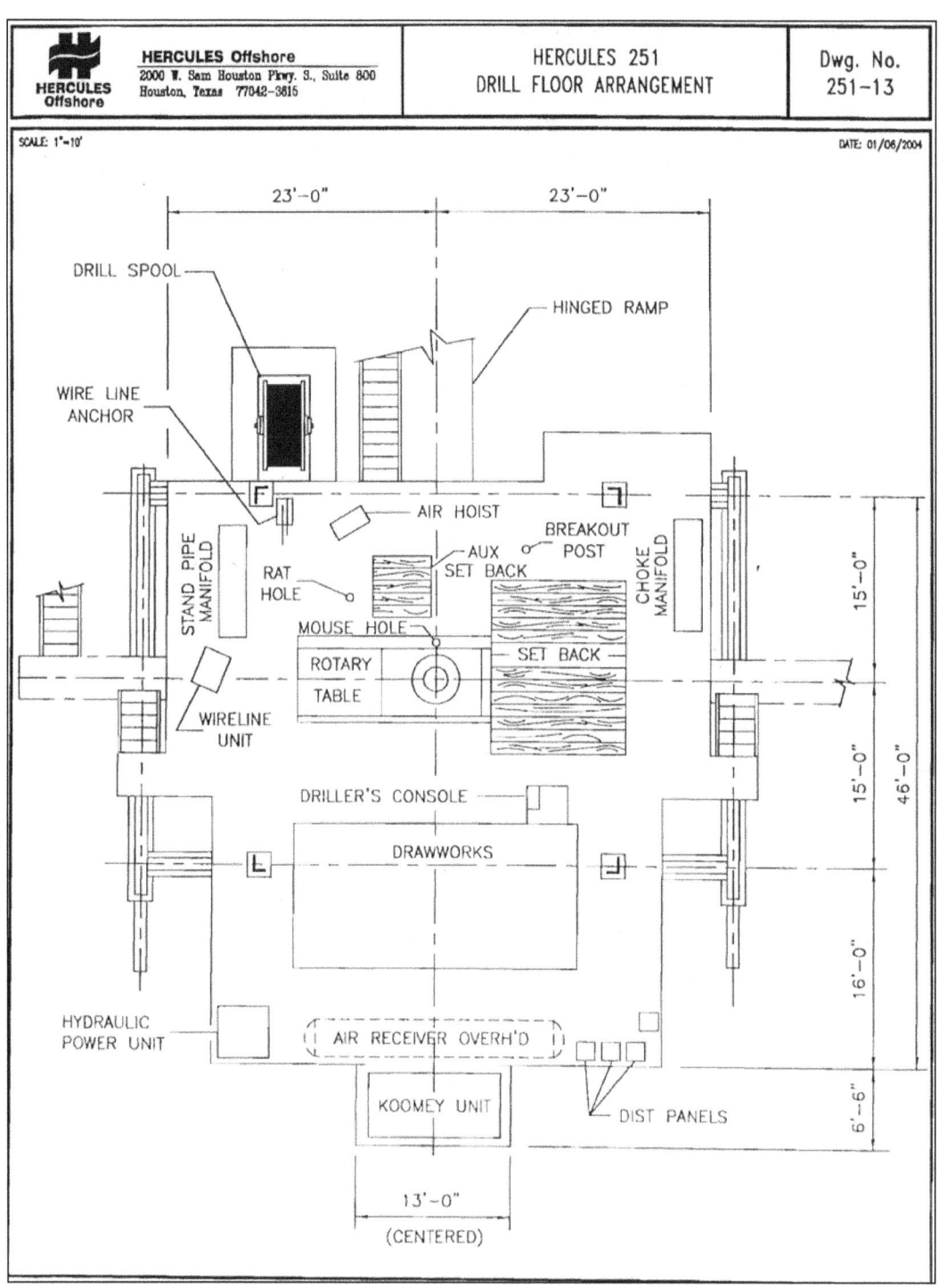

HERCULES Offshore
2000 W. Sam Houston Pkwy. S., Suite 800
Houston, Texas 77042-3615

HERCULES 251
DRILL FLOOR ARRANGEMENT

Dwg. No.
251-13

SCALE: 1"=10'

DATE: 01/06/2004

23'-0"

23'-0"

DRILL SPOOL

HINGED RAMP

WIRE LINE
ANCHOR

STAND PIPE MANIFOLD

AIR HOIST

BREAKOUT
POST

CHOKE MANIFOLD

RAT
HOLE

AUX
SET BACK

MOUSE HOLE

ROTARY
TABLE

SET BACK

15'-0"

WIRELINE
UNIT

15'-0"

46'-0"

DRILLER'S CONSOLE

DRAWWORKS

16'-0"

HYDRAULIC
POWER UNIT

AIR RECEIVER OVERH'D

6'-6"

KOOMEY UNIT

DIST PANELS

13'-0"

(CENTERED)

Figure 3 – Floor plan of Hercules Rig 251

8

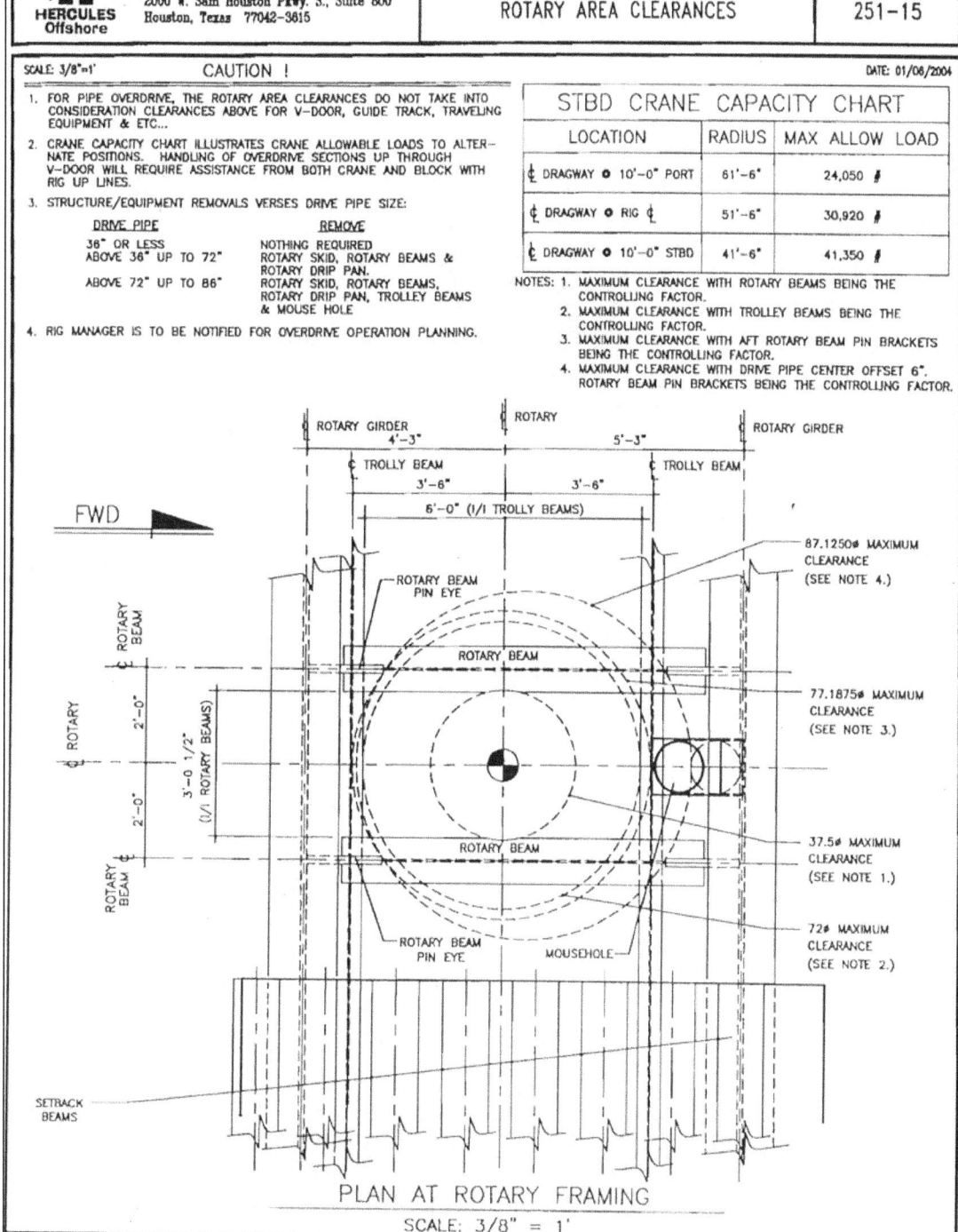

Figure 4: Rotary area clearances

0715-hrs: Two Frank's personnel continued to cut the oil pan under the supervision of the Welding Supervisor (*see figure 5*). The Derrickman approached a Frank's personnel (unidentified) and repeated the Driller's previous admonition to refrain from cutting the Oil Pan. Other Hercules personnel continued maintenance and other operations on the Rig floor to ready the Rig to pickup and run 60-inch drive pipe.

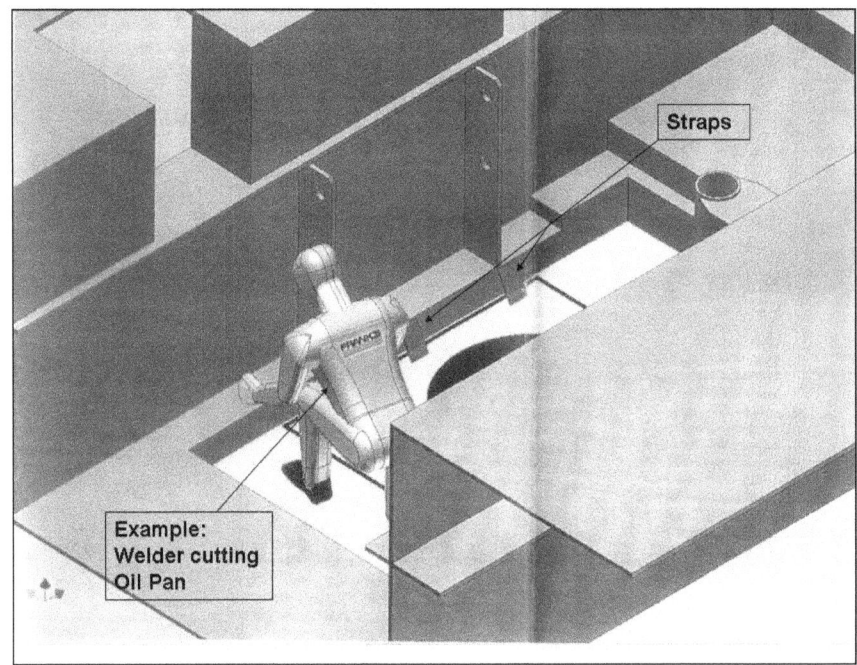

Figure 5 – Diagram of position of a welder while cutting oil pan (graphics from Frank's)

0725-hrs: One of the Frank's personnel working in the Oil Pan, Welder #2, requested that fall protection be acquired so that when the cut was finished the two welders would be protected. He also requested a "tugger" connected to an air hoist be provided to support the pan upon completion of the cut. The Rig Derrickman sent a Hercules floorman to get the fall protection gear.

0729-hrs: Welder #2 told the Welding Supervisor that he felt something was wrong with the operation and that perhaps the job should be suspended. No job stoppage occurred. Welder #2 stepped out of the Oil Pan onto one of the support beams while the Welder #1 continued to cut his portion of the Oil Pan.

0733-hrs: The Welder #1 continued cutting another of the metal straps that needed to be removed to complete the opening in the Oil Pan. Without warning the entire Oil Pan suddenly dropped downward hinging on the side being cut by Welder #2 (*see figure 6*), and then almost immediately fell away from beneath the two welders working on the cut.

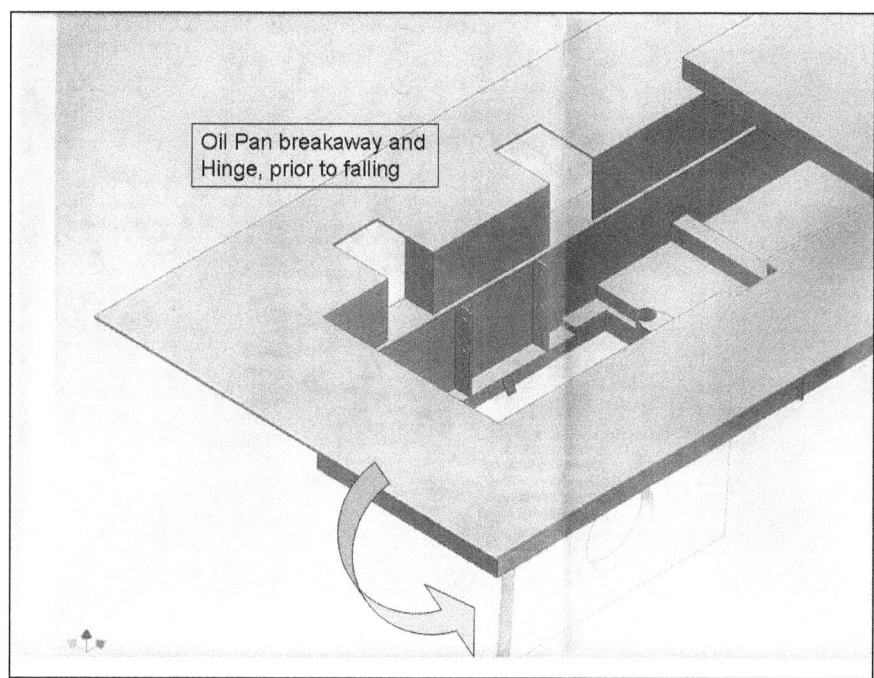

Oil Pan breakaway and Hinge, prior to falling

Figure 6 – Diagram showing how the oil pan hinged, and then fell (graphics from Frank's)

Just prior to the Oil Pan fall, Welder #2 had stepped out of the Oil Pan onto one of the beams that bordered the Oil Pan. When the Oil Pan fell away, he was able to maintain his already established foot position on the beam and using hand holds higher on the side of the Rotary Table Well, he was able to prevent himself from falling after the Oil Pan.

The Welder #1 who had continued to cut the Oil Pan after Welder #2 had stepped out, attempted to grab a hand hold on a sub-structure beam along the side of the Rotary Table Well as the Oil Pan fell. He was able to momentarily hold onto a beam but shortly lost his handhold and fell after the Oil Pan. He struck the Wellhead and/or the Texas Deck some 50-ft below the Rig floor, then continued to fall, finally landing in the Gulf of Mexico (*see figures 7 and 8*).

Figure 7 – End location of the oil pan and pallet on the Texas deck

Figure 8 – View down through the rotary table well after fall of the oil pan

0734-hrs: The Derrickman, hearing the Oil Pan fall and seeing the Welder #1 go into the water, immediately sounded the alarm and threw a life preserver to the overboard man. He ran to the life capsule and with two other Hercules hands, immediately initiated launch of the capsule. A Hercules floorman ran down to the Texas deck and another went to inform the OIM in his office of the Accident.

The Derrickman maneuvered the life capsule to recover the overboard Welder #1 who was floating face down. Within 15 minutes the Welder #1 was recovered into the capsule and then transferred back the rig floor. Though no signs of life were observed, respiration and other first aid measures were initiated in the capsule and continued for approximately 20 minutes on the Rig with no sign of revival of the Welder #1. Efforts to revive the Welder #1 were discontinued after the Rig first responder medic conferred with Coast Guard personnel and concluded continued efforts to revive the Welder #1 were futile.

1000-hrs: An Air-med helicopter transported Welder #1 to Galveston where the County of Galveston Medical Examiners Office found the him to be deceased on arrival. Primary cause was described as "blunt force injuries"

Preparation of the Rig Floor and Removal of the Oil Pollution Pan

The objective of the operation underway when the Accident occurred was to install 60-inch drive pipe over a completed well to support a caisson platform deck. The Operator planned to install equipment on the caisson deck to allow the well to be placed on remote production.

To install drive pipe of this size, it was necessary to prepare the rig floor in the usual manner, including removing the rotary table, skid, rotary beams, modifying the structure, and installing false rotary beams to support the running of the drive pipe, etc. In addition to these modifications, drive pipe of this size also required the removal or modification of the Oil Pan.

The Oil Pan installed on the Rig could accommodate drive pipe up to 36-inches without modification. Larger pipe would require its removal. The Oil Pan was installed about 6-ft beneath the rotary table. It was tray-shaped, approximately 9'7" x 5'7" and approximately 8-inches deep (*see figure 9*). Because of the nature of the sub-structure of the Rig, the top edges of the Oil Pan "tray" were not visible from inside the Rotary Table Well. The view of those edges was blocked by sub-structure beams.

Figure 9 – Dimensions and view of the oil pollution pan

According to testimony from several of the Frank's crew including the Welding Supervisor, the method of attaching an oil pollution pan beneath a rotary table varies on each rig. However all the Frank's crew testified that they had never encountered an oil pan whose outside edges were not either completely welded to the rig around their outside diameter, or was bolted firmly to the rig sub-structure.

Removing an oil pollution pan usually requires cutting the pan away from the rig sub-structure or unbolting it and removing it with a block. According to testimony by the Frank's crew, when rigging up to run large sized drive pipe the usual method of modifying the pan to allow the pipe to pass is to cut a hole in the pan large enough to accommodate the drive pipe diameter. After the drive pipe operation was completed, the hole would then be welded shut restoring the fluid-tight integrity of the oil pan.

According to testimony, the Oil Pan of the Rig was attached in a different manner from that usually encountered on other rigs. The Oil Pan was not hard-welded around the lips of its sides, nor was it bolted to the rig sub-structure. Instead, it was attached to the Rig sub-structure beams by means of six metal straps (Straps) that were welded to the bottom of the Oil Pan, and then individually welded to substructure beams (*see figure 10 and 11*).

14

Figure 10 – View of the location of some strap welds on the oil pan

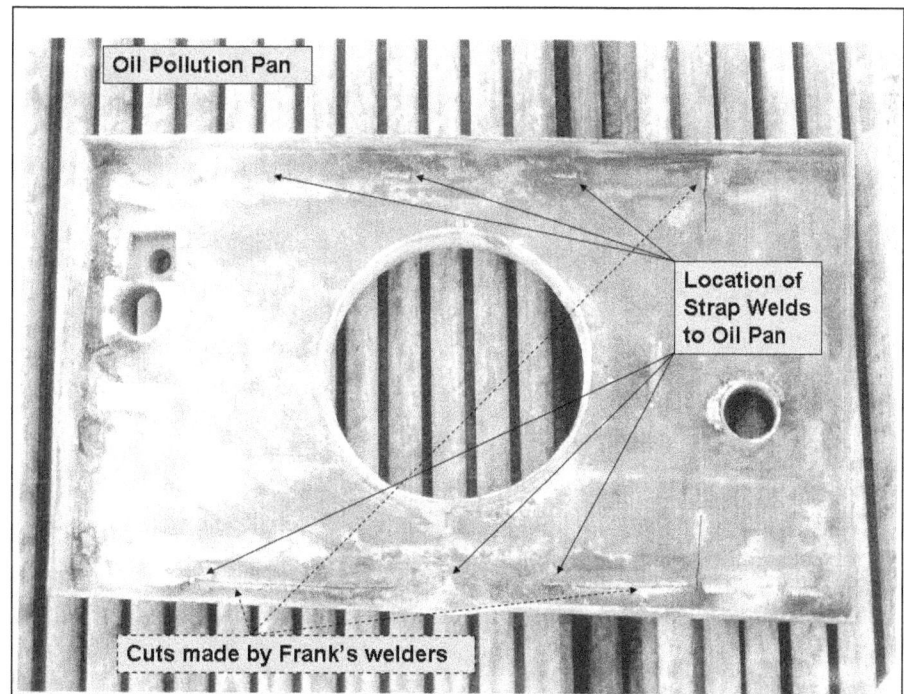

Figure 11 – Top view of oil pan showing cuts and some strap weld locations

One result of attaching the Oil Pan in this manner was that it made the removal of the pan easier than would be the case if the pan's side edges were completely welded to the Rig. Because of the routing of the sub-structure beams, cutting out the entire pan would have to be approached from beneath the Rig floor and would require some relatively complex method of supporting the welders. However, by attaching the pan with Straps, the removal could be accomplished by simply cutting those Straps. Then the pan could be "snaked" out through the Rotary Table Well.

Frank's Personnel Initial Actions: Testimony

From testimony, the Frank's crew arrived on the Rig approximately *2300-hrs* on *Jan 28*. After being assigned bunks and briefed on the Rig evacuation plan, the Crew had a maximum of about 2-3 hours of rest before beginning work. According to testimony, the boat trip out had encountered some relatively rough weather and some of the crew had commuted up to 10 hours before arriving at the dock. It is unknown how much rest members of the Frank's crew had prior to beginning the drive pipe operation.

For the Frank's personnel, the operation was supposed to consist of preparing the Rig substructure to hold the false rotary beams, removing the Oil Pan, installing the false rotary beams, and then initiating the major portion of the work, the installation of the 60-inch drive pipe.

Testimony from several of Frank's personnel on site when the Accident occurred indicated that none of the Frank's personnel attended any JSA-think plan meeting held by the Rig Night Tool Pusher or supervisory personnel. Instead, a preliminary meeting was conducted by the Frank's Welding Supervisor to review the details of the operation. Testimony indicated that in that meeting the Franks crew discussed the dangers inherent in the job, focusing especially on pinch points, fall protection, welding equipment, etc. No discussion of the methodology of removing the Oil Pan was included in their safety meeting other than a statement that the pan would be "cut out." No signed JSA form was generated and no written record of the meeting, its agenda, or who attended was created.

Testimony from the Welding Supervisor indicated that neither he nor any other Frank's personnel conducted a preliminary investigation into the way the Oil Pan was attached to the Rig sub-structure.

Documents were received indicating that various crews from Frank's had conducted casing operations on board the Rig four separate times in 2006-8 prior to the Accident. None of those jobs involved installing drive pipe and none of those jobs had required removal or modification of the Oil Pan.

Hercules Rig Personnel Initial Actions, JSA: Testimony

According to morning reports and testimony of several members of the Rig crew, the Night Tool Pusher conducted a JSA-think plan safety meeting prior to the start of the drive pipe operation at about *0500-hrs.* Attendance was not mandatory and none of the Frank's personnel were at the meeting. A JSA form was not completed and signed by attendees during the meeting and it is unknown if the Rig welder was at the meeting.

According to testimony from various members of the Hercules personnel, the upcoming drive pipe operation was discussed at the meeting, with emphasis on the dangers and steps involved in the actual welding and running the drive pipe string. The testimony indicated that the preparation of the Rig floor prior to picking up the first joint of 60-inch drive pipe was not discussed in detail possibly because much of the preliminary work was already completed. Because the Frank's personnel were not at the meeting, there was no introduction of supervisory personnel from the two companies to each other.

Testimony was received that no discussion of the methodology for removing the Oil Pan was addressed in the Rig think plan JSA meeting. The Driller testified that he thought the Rig personnel on tower had been assigned responsibility for removing the Oil Pan. The Derrickman testified he thought the Rig welder was going to personally remove the Oil Pan. He testified that the Rig welder had been assigned to the Rig for several years and was very experienced and knowledgeable about how the Oil Pan was attached.

It was later discovered during testimony that the Rig welder who had been working on the Rig for several years, and whom the Derrickman believed was the person with the knowledge and responsibility to remove the Oil Pan, had left the Rig two days previously. His replacement was a newer, less experienced employee who had not been on the Rig before. The replacement Rig welder was not present on the Rig floor during the time of the Accident. Testimony was received that one of the Hercules personnel thought he was in bed, though that was not confirmed. It is not known if the replacement Rig welder knew how the Oil Pan was secured by Straps to the Rig sub-structure.

Testimony was received from the Driller and Derrickman that they did not know who the supervisor for the Frank's crew was. They assumed that the Hammer Operator was the man in charge of Frank's personnel because *"that is who is usually in charge of drive pipe crews."* The Driller testified that he did not know if he or the Frank's supervisor was supposed to run the detailed aspects of the job. He testified that he thought he and his men were charged with removing the Oil Pan, with the help of the Rig welder.

Hercules Rig Personnel Actions through Accident: Testimony

At *0500-hrs* when the Frank's crew began preparing the Rig floor for the installation of the beams for the false rotary, the Hercules crew on tower became engaged in other "housekeeping" tasks. The OIM who relieved the Night Tool Pusher came onto the Rig floor for considerable time from approximately *0600-hrs* to about *0620-hrs*. According to his testimony, during that time he engaged the Frank's Welding Supervisor in an extended conversation about the upcoming operation and other subjects.

He reported that the Frank's Welding Supervisor briefed him on the plans for the drive pipe operation. He could not recall if he specifically discussed the Oil Pan but did recall the subject being mentioned. He indicated that he believed that the Hercules personnel would remove the Oil Pan but was not sure if he transmitted that information to the Frank's Welding Supervisor. He testified that while he did not explicitly know how the Oil Pan was attached to the sub-structure, he had relied upon the Rig welder to deal with that piece of equipment in the past. He could not recall the last time the Oil Pan had been removed but believed that it had been over a year since that operation was necessary.

Testimony from the Driller, OIM, and Frank's Welding Supervisor agreed that the OIM did not introduce the Driller to the Frank's Welding Supervisor or include the Driller in the discussion he had with the Welding Supervisor about the upcoming operation. The OIM testified that he was not aware that the Driller and Frank's Welding Supervisor were unclear about their respective responsibilities or that they were not in routine communication and coordinating their actions with each other.

The Driller testified that he knew that the Oil Pan was connected to the Rig floor only by the Straps. He believed that the Rig welder was assigned to remove the Oil Pan after the installation of the false rotary beams. He thought that the Frank's crew was only supposed to prepare the substructure and install the beams for the false rotary, not remove the Oil Pan. He and his assistant, the Derrickman, were supervising cleaning the Rig floor while the Frank's crew prepared for the installation of their beams.

The Driller testified that he discovered that no hot work permit had been signed prior to the start of the work. He retrieved a copy of a previous hot work permit and filled in the details according to what he remembered was covered in the meeting. He testified that he did not know who the supervisor for the Frank's crew actually was and had not spoken to him or coordinated the plans for modifying the Rig floor with him. However, he sought out the person he thought was the lead supervisor of Frank's personnel, the Hammer Operator, and had him sign the hot work forms.

The Driller testified that he believed that the Hammer Operator was the lead supervisor for the Frank's Crew because it was his understanding that the hammer man is usually the head of a drive pipe operation. Later, as the OIM finished his conversation with the Frank's Welding Supervisor and was leaving the Rig floor, the Driller testified that he briefly spoke with the OIM about the ongoing operation and was left with the impression that he and the Hercules floor personnel would be responsible for removing the Oil Pan, and that would occur after the Frank's crew had completed the installation of the false rotary support beams.

He testified that his conversation with the OIM did not result in a clear set of instructions in part because of the "rambling nature of the conversation" with the OIM. The Driller testified that in the past he had encountered some difficulty understanding exactly what was expected of him due to that characteristic way of communicating instructions by the OIM.

Approximately at *0700-hrs*, the Driller and Derrickman both testified that they noticed Frank's welders descending into the Rotary Table Well with their welding equipment. They then noticed the welders had drawn a chalk line on the Oil Pan and had started to cut out the Oil Pan using welding torches. The Driller testified that he approached the Hammer Operator who he thought was the Frank's supervisor, and told him to tell the welders to quit cutting the Oil Pan.

19

The Hammer Operator testified that he thought he recalled the incident, but may not have understood the urgency as there was no mention that cutting the Oil Pan jeopardized the integrity of its attachment to the Rig sub-structure. The Driller testified that he did not give a reason for his desire to stop the cutting in part because he thought he [the Driller] was the responsible authority for events on the Rig floor. Therefore, he merely told the Frank's personnel to stop, but, he did not talk to the actual Frank's supervisor and/or explain the request.

Approximately 20 minutes later, the Driller and Derrickman testified that they again noticed that Frank's welders were working on the Oil Pan. The Derrickman approached one of the Frank's crewmen (unidentified) and told him that Frank's welders needed to stop cutting on the Oil Pan. He testified that he did not give the reason but assumed that they would follow the instructions of the Driller and Rig floor personnel. The Hammer Operator testified that he thought he told the Welding Supervisor that the Driller had mentioned a desire for the welders to quit working on the Oil Pan, but did not give him a reason.

Frank's Personnel Actions through the Accident: Testimony

At approximately *0600-hrs*, the Welding Supervisor testified that the OIM approached him on the Rig floor. He reported that they were old acquaintances. They had a relatively long conversation, 10-20 minutes, about the upcoming drive pipe operation and other personal matters.

The Welding Supervisor testified that he thought he had fully described his plans to the OIM. He indicated he talked about his plans to cut a hole in the Oil Pan large enough to accommodate the 60-inch drive pipe after he had completed preparing the sub-structure to receive the false rotary support beams. He testified that he remembered that the OIM had asked him if he "had enough room" to modify the Rig sub-structure to allow running the 60-inch pipe. He recalled pointing to the dimensions of the Oil Pan that were visible and accessible and noting the 66-inches between the sub-structure beams. He testified that he remembered thinking that he could cut out a square approximately 64-inches per side that would give ample room to run the 60-inch pipe without having to modify the sub-structure beams. He did not recall receiving any instructions from the OIM that the Rig crew would handle removing the Oil Pan.

The Welding Supervisor testified that he did not recall being told by the Driller or other Hercules personnel to cease cutting operations in the Oil Pan during the time immediately preceding the Accident.

According to testimony of Welder #2, he and the Welder #1 descended onto the top of the Oil Pan after the completion of the preparation of the sub-structure to receive the false rotary beams. He testified that he and Welder #1 were instructed by the Welding Supervisor to cut out the Oil Pan in a square approximately 64-inches on a side. He testified that they drew a line on the Oil Pan. After the initial corner cuts were made he noticed several metal straps welded to both the bottom of the Oil Pan and to the sub structure beams. He indicated to the Welding Supervisor that those straps would have to be cut to make an opening large enough to accommodate the 60-inch drive pipe.

Testimony from the Welder #2 and the Welding Supervisor was received that fall protection was not provided to the two welders working in the Oil Pan because it was assumed that the Pan formed a solid floor. The distance from the Rig Floor to the bottom of the Oil Pan was approximately 6-ft... but that included several "steps" and it did not seem to the Welding Supervisor to require fall protection. The 39-inch diameter hole in the center of the Oil Pan was covered with an unsecured pallet during the cutting operation. Testimony was received that this was intended to prevent the welders from inadvertently falling through that opening.

Welder #2 testified that the Welding Supervisor was in something of a hurry to complete the set up and begin the drive pipe operation. He noted that he was working on one side of the Oil Pan while the Welder #1 was working on the other. He did not recall any instructions to allow the Hercules crew to remove the Oil Pan nor did he remember seeing other members of the Frank's crew except the Hammer Operator.

After the initial cuts were made in the bottom of the Oil Pan, Welder #2 testified that he began to feel uneasy about the security of the platform after he cut one of the Straps. He testified that he felt the Oil Pan give a little and it seemed to wobble when the two welders moved about. He stopped working while Welder #1 continued to cut his side, moving ahead somewhat faster than Welder #2. Welder #2 testified that he told the Welding Supervisor that something was wrong and he did not feel comfortable continuing to work without fall protection. He also testified that he was concerned that as the cuts progressed the center section should be supported by the air hoist and he requested a line be made available.

According to testimony of Welder #2, the Welding Supervisor told him to continue to cut his side of the Oil Pan and that the he, the Welding Supervisor, would determine when fall protection was required. The Welding Supervisor however testified that he requested a Hercules Rig employee retrieve the fall protection. He also said he requested a line from an air hoist to be readied. The Derrickman later testified that he sent someone to retrieve the fall protection gear.

Shortly afterward, Welder #2 testified that he again told the Welding Supervisor that he no longer felt safe continuing to work in the Oil Pan and that he was going to stop. He then said he stepped out of the Oil Pan onto one of the support beams and that the Welding Supervisor instructed him to continue to work while the requested gear was rigged up.

The Welding Supervisor testified that he first thought Welder #2 was simply concerned with getting the fall protection and air hoist ready so that when the cuts were finished they would be available. He said he did not believe that Welder #2 had intended to initiate a "stop work" course of action even though he may have said something about halting his part of the work momentarily.

When Welder #2 stopped working and stepped out of the Oil Pan, the Welding Supervisor testified that he then told Welder #2 to instruct Welder #1 to cease work until the fall protection gear was obtained. He testified that the environment was pretty noisy so that he was unsure whether Welder #2 had understood him. Welder #2 testified that he was not told to halt Welder #1's work. However he took it upon himself to tell Welder #1 that he thought they should stop their work because something was not right, but that Welder #1 ignored him and continued cutting the Straps and Oil Pan on his side.

At approximately *0733-hrs*, Welder #2 testified that he was standing on a Rig floor sub-structure support beam just above the Oil Pan. Welder #1 was continuing to cut the Straps and Oil Pan on his side of the Rotary Table Well. The Derrickman (according to his testimony) was involved getting the fall protection. The Welding Supervisor was observing the progress of the cutting operation. Two other members of Frank's crew were either directly observing or continuing to prepare to install the false rotary beams.

Suddenly the Oil Pan dropped away like a giant hinge, opening beneath the Welder #1 and hinging on the side of Welder #2. Almost immediately thereafter, the Oil Pan broke free from the rig sub-structure and fell approximately 50 ft, landing on the Texas deck next to the wellhead (*see figure 7, p. 12*).

Welder #2 testified that because he had his feet on a support beam when the Oil Pan fell he was able to use his legs to support his body until he found a hand hold saving himself from falling after the Oil Pan. He testified that the Welder #1 grabbed one of the sub-structure support beams as the Oil Pan dropped from beneath him. However the beam was slippery with oil residue and the Welder #1 was unable to maintain his hold.

Hercules and Frank's JSA Requirements and Stop Work Policy

Frank's Safety Management System Manual (FSMS) provides employees with general guidelines for implementing a standard for safety. Several sections detail the steps to be fully planned before initiating hammer operations. A sample JSA form is included in the FSMS, listing the main hazards usually encountered that should be discussed at the JSA meeting. While fall protection, pinch points, welding procedures, safety considerations using cranes and scaffolds, etc. are all recommended to be addressed in detail at the JSA meeting, the FSMS in effect when the Accident occurred nowhere mentioned anything about the removal of Oil Pollution Pans from beneath the rotary.

Regarding the FSMS policy for "stop work," Section 12 of the FSMS defines the purpose, scope, definition and responsibility of the Stop Work Authority (SWA) program. Section 4.3.1 states that, "*Line Supervisors are responsible to condone a culture where SWA is exercised freely, honor request for stop work, work to resolve issues before operations resume and recognize proactive participation.*"

Portions of Section 12 noted that all employees, "*...have the authority and obligation to stop any task or operation where concerns or questions regarding... risk exists.*" The procedure for SWA defined in Section 12 requires that when a person identifies a perceived unsafe condition... he should coordinate the stop work through the supervisor. If the supervisor is not available, he should initiate the stop work himself directly with those at risk. Section SMS-P-4.2.08 instructs the employee initiating SWA to start by "*introducing [himself] and starting a conversation with the phrase 'I am using my stop work authority because...'*"

23

Section 4.3.2 for Safety Observation states that, "*Line supervisors shall investigate every reported safety observation and take steps to eliminate the hazard or if elimination is not possible, take steps to reduce the hazard to As Low As Reasonably Practical (ALARP).*" Section 4.3.1 of the FSMS for PPE Awareness states that, "*The line supervisor shall ensure that the tasks within his/her department have been assessed and that PPE requirements identified are obtained, distributed and training given.*"

The FSMS current at the time of the Accident did not designate a hand signal or visual way to initiate a SWA in the event of a chaotic or noisy environment.

The Hercules Rig HSE Manual in effect at the time of the accident was a hold-over from the acquisition of TODCO (previous owner-operator of the Rig) by Hercules some months previously. The manual did not discuss the specific requirements for fall protection to be used during inspection or work in or on an oil pollution pan. The manual made no specific mention of a requirement for all involved in an operation to attend a pre-job JSA or "think plan" meeting. Testimony by the OIM indicated that such attendance is normally a unanimously attended event but that it was not an absolute requirement.

Conclusions

The Accident

On January 28, 2008, at approximately 0730-hours, a casing crew was modifying the Rig floor in preparation for running 60-inch drive pipe. Two welders began working in the Rotary Table Well, atop the Oil Pan, using a welding torch to cut a hole in the Oil Pan large enough to allow the passage of the drive pipe.

In order to create an opening large enough to pass the drive pipe, the welders found that it was necessary to cut six steel "straps" attached to the surface of the Oil Pan and also welded to the side of the sub-structure support beams. After a number of the straps were cut the Oil Pan abruptly fell free, dropping approximately 50-ft before landing on the Texas deck. When the Oil Pan dropped away, one of the welders working in the pan also fell striking the wellhead and/or the Texas deck before landing in the Gulf of Mexico. The fall resulted in a fatal injury to the welder.

Cause of Fatality

(1) The Straps were the only connection holding the Oil Pan in place. Therefore, cutting the straps allowed the Oil Pan to fall out from beneath the welders.

(2) Neither the welding supervisor nor the welders knew the straps were the only support for the Oil Pan and no one had reviewed the set up before cutting the pan. They assumed the entire top edge of the Oil Pan was welded to the Rig sub-structure and formed a solid floor.

(3) Because of the above assumption, the welders working in the Oil Pan were not wearing fall protection.

(4) Planning for the operation was inadequate, and were not conducted according to Rig or Contractor policy.

- None of the Contractor crew and only part of Rig personnel attended the JSA/think plan meeting;

25

- The planning meetings that were held were not comprehensive. Neither the Rig JSA meeting nor the Contractor pre-job meeting discussed the removal of the Oil Pollution Pan in detail.

- Rig company policy was not followed. None of the following Permit to Work form items were accomplished prior to initiating the work, despite being checked off and signed as being completed:

  - *"Has the complete plan for safely conducting the work the work been effectively communicated to each person who will be performing this work?"*
  - *"Does everyone understand the plan, their part in the plan and the controls required?"*
  - *"Have all persons who may be affected by this work been adequately informed of the consequences and any precautions required?"*

(5) Communication was inadequate at several levels:

- A discussion of the operation between the *OIM and the Welding Supervisor* while work was underway failed to identify how the pan was attached to the sub-structure. The proper method for removing the pan was not communicated adequately nor understood by all parties.

- The *OIM and Driller/Rig floor* personnel did not understand how the Frank's contractor planned to proceed with the work. The Driller thought the Rig Welder was going to remove the oil pan under his (the Driller's) supervision, while the OIM had discussed the modification with the Welding Supervisor who believed his personnel were responsible.

- The *Hercules floor personnel* including the Driller did not know who the supervisor in charge of the *Frank's crew and work was* and therefore communicated the request to halt the cutting of the oil pan to the wrong person. The *Driller* failed to communicate the imminent danger of the Oil Pan falling when the straps were cut in words that were understood by the appropriate person(s) on the *Contractor crew*.

- The communication between the *Welder #2* in the oil pan and the *Welding Supervisor* failed to initiate "stop work" prior to the accident. The *Welding Supervisor* did not understand *Welder #2's* request to "stop work" and his sense of the existence of a dangerous condition.

- The *OIM* failed to inform the *Driller* who was responsible for removal of the pan nor did he clarify role responsibilities by clearly defining the goals for the Frank's crew.

(6) Supervision was inadequate on all levels:

- The *Rig management* failed to conduct a fully attended JSA meeting that discussed the various components of the casing operation as required by company policy, despite the Permit to Work form.

- The *Rig management* failed to fully discuss the details of the operation during a direct conversation with the Frank's *Welding Supervisor*, and failed to check that the procedure adopted by the Contractor was proper.

- The *Rig management* failed to inform all the crews of the Rig and Contractor who the supervisors of each sub-operation were.

- The Frank's *Welding Supervisor* failed to evaluate the details of the rig floor sub-structure and the connection of the oil pan prior to beginning work.

- The Frank's *Welding Supervisor* failed to discuss or clear the details of his plan with the *Driller* and with the *Rig Supervisor* (s) in a way that defined his intentions.

- The Franks *Welding Supervisor* failed to insure a full understanding of the methodology of the stop-work plan by his workers. He failed to comprehend and/or communicate the need to "stop work" when the potential for danger was indicated by *Welder #2*.

- The *Driller* (Rig floor supervisor) failed to insure a unified Contractor/Rig plan on the floor before work was begun. The *Rig floor supervisors* failed to identify the supervisory personnel of Contractor.

- The need for fall protection was not addressed by supervisors or managers despite work heights and the extreme potential results involved with any fall during the oil pan removal.

Probable Contributing Causes

The Contractor Company (and Rig Company) failed to insure that a method of initiating a "*stop-work*" action was in place and fully understood by all crew members. A common methodology for initiating "*stop-work*" was probably not communicated during the initial Rig orientation meeting when the Contractor crew first boarded the Rig, nor was it identified in the safety manuals.

Possible Contributing Causes

It is possible that the fact that no guidelines or standard procedures for removing or modifying an oil pan was included in either the Rig Company or Contractor Company operational manuals contributed to the cause of the Accident. It is possible that neither company had conducted training for their crews that reviewed the different types of oil pans and the methods for removing them.

The time line of mobilization for the Contractor crew suggests the possibility that fatigue could have contributed to some of the inattention to details by Contractor supervisors and crew that led to this accident.

Recommendations

It is recommended that MMS consider issuing Safety Alert (s) that briefly describes the fatal accident and alerts the operators to the following:

1. *Supervisors and rig managers should be aware of the need to carefully examine the method by which the oil pollution pans are attached prior to initiating any operation to modify or remove them.*

2. *Rig managers should insure an unambiguous chain of command for any work involving contractors on the rig floor. Rig managers should require all contract personnel to attend a pre-job JSA meeting and should insure that the supervisors of all elements know who their counterparts are.*

3. *The operators, all service companies including rig companies, and third-party contractors, should review their methods of initiating a "stop-work" event to insure that the system adopted will actually be effective under job conditions. The companies should insure that a hand signal method to "stop-work" is available for those situations where time and job circumstances do not allow conventional conversation.*

4. *The Operators and all service companies and contractors should consider emphasizing in their training that inadequate, incomplete communications remains one of the most common causes of major accidents.*

www.ingramcontent.com/pod-product-compliance
Lightning Source LLC
Chambersburg PA
CBHW052025280526

45793CB00005B/1133